Our Place in His Story

Gavin Reid

 bible reading fellowship

Text copyright © 1994 Gavin Reid and Shelagh Brown

Published by
The Bible Reading Fellowship
Peter's Way
Sandy Lane West
Oxford
OX4 5HG
ISBN 0 7459 2593 6
Albatross Books Pty Ltd
PO Box 320
Sutherland
NSW 2232
Australia
ISBN 0 7324 0800 8

First edition 1994

Scripture quotations are taken from the
Holy Bible, New International Version,
copyright © 1973, 1978, 1984 by
International Bible Society. Used by permission.
Illustrations by Mark Cripps

A catalogue record for this book is available
from the British Library

Printed in Great Britain
by Cox & Wyman Ltd., Reading

Contents

Introduction

TV's most popular programmes are the soap operas. They draw huge audiences and we keep coming back for more!

Why do the soaps have such an appeal? Almost certainly because they strike a chord in all of us. They are about ongoing stories and all of us know that we ourselves are in the middle of ongoing stories. The difference from the soaps is that the stories we are involved in are *true*!

There are two sorts of stories in which we find ourselves involved. There are, first, those stories about which we have no choice. I did not choose my parents. I didn't arrange for them to meet. I didn't choose their nationality. I am caught up in the ongoing story of the Reid family and the British nation.

We also get involved, however, in a second sort of story. This is the story where we don't have to be involved but where we choose to be. When I married my wife we both chose to start—as it were—telling a new story together. I not only entered into the true-life 'soap opera' of her parents and relatives and history; she chose to enter mine. The Reid family story goes on and she is part of it. The Smith family story goes on, and I am part of that.

This booklet is about what I believe to be the greatest story of all time. It is about a story that started the day the world began. Its chief character lived twenty centuries ago in the Middle East. His name is Jesus of Nazareth, or Jesus the Christ. But this story isn't only about the past. For me, and for millions like me, it is about the present and the future. The episodes in this true life 'soap' are still being written and episodes are planned for every day until the end of time. There has been, is now, and will be, a cast of millions. The storyline deals with the greatest truth of all time—that we human beings are not alone. We came from somewhere and someone. We are going somewhere. And

6

someone bigger than all of us cares deeply about us every day. That someone is writing in the details of the plot and he is ready to write in everyone who wants to be part of the story. We call that someone—*God*.

But all this is jumping ahead. We need to go back twenty centuries to the heart of the story.

The Story of Jesus

Most of us have heard something about the story of Jesus—it's been around for a long time. The trouble with something that's been around a long time is that people stop taking it seriously. It becomes part of the wallpaper of life.

There are four accounts of his life which date back to his times. They are written under the names of Matthew, Mark, Luke and John. They tell very little about Jesus before he was about thirty. It seems that he had worked in the family carpentry business after growing up just like any other youngster of his time. What little is on record of his birth and childhood, however, suggests that there was something out of the ordinary about him. His mother, Mary, was well aware of this.

One day it all started happening. He left the carpenter's workshop and began to gather followers. There was something about him that made a deep impression on people. 'Follow me—I'll make you people who fish for men!' was what he said to a group of men who earned their living from fishing. Somehow, he didn't need to say any more! They left their boats and tackle (and their livelihood) and they were off.

The buzz was soon around the region. There was a new teacher, well worth hearing. 'Could he,' asked some, 'be the

Christ our forefathers said would come?' 'Was he going to lead a revolution against the occupying Roman authorities?'

Jesus taught about God and what life was supposed to mean. He said that God is more than a far away, lofty something-or-other. He is *our Father*. God's will lies behind the existence of each one of us. We matter to him.

He taught that God is the true ruler or 'King' of the universe. While other powers may seem to be in charge and other kingdoms have had their day—all history was heading for a final showdown when the Father and the King would also be the Judge.

Wherever Jesus went the crowds gathered and strange things happened. People with illnesses were healed. He gave sight to blind people. He made those who were deaf hear again. He touched cripples and they were straightened and strengthened. On one occasion he brought a dead man back to life. All four accounts of the story of Jesus agree on these amazing claims.

But there was another side to the story. Wherever he went, the nasty side of life revealed itself. Those writing at the time spoke of people being demon-possessed. The very presence of Jesus seemed to bring this frightening reality into the open. In some way Jesus was able to drive out the demons.

The whole question of evil, of selfishness, of a basic built-in wrongness in people's lives was never far from his teaching. He was constantly saying that people needed to

be forgiven—put right with each other and with God himself. Being religious was not enough in itself. It could all too easily become an excuse for not facing up to the need to receive God's forgiveness. This angered many of the religious leaders of the day. He was a threat. He exposed their hypocrisy. They began to make plans for his arrest.

There were other people wanting someone to lead an armed rebellion against the Romans. They were disappointed. Jesus said that it was the gentle not the powerful who would end up 'inheriting the land'. The way of life he taught was a way of gentleness and love. Someone asked, 'How often should I forgive my neighbour for sinning against me—till seven times?' 'No,' Jesus replied. 'Until seventy-times seven!'

He spoke of relying on God to provide the power when it was needed. These were hardly the words of the national leader they were looking for. What made matters worse was that Jesus treated the Romans as he treated everyone else—as people who mattered.

Eventually the enemies of Jesus joined forces. At a great religious festival in Jerusalem when large crowds had gathered and feelings were running high, Jesus arrived dramatically and began to teach in the capital itself. Opposition groups tried to catch him out with trick questions but the crisis came when Jesus was praying in a quiet park one evening, accompanied by two or three of his closest followers. His whereabouts had been made known to the authorities by one of his followers, who had been bribed to give such information. Soldiers arrived and arrested him. He went quietly and calmly.

Within hours a hastily convened court had pronounced him guilty of blasphemy (claiming to be God). To the people of Judea that was a capital offence. The Roman authorities were persuaded to let the death sentence go ahead. By now rabble rousers had stirred up the huge crowds in Jerusalem to shout for his execution.

Jesus was flogged, made to carry a large spar of wood to the public execution place, nailed to it and hung up to die while jeering crowds watched. Very few of what had once been a large group of followers were standing by him at the end. His last word—according to John's account—was one which means 'Completed!'. But *what* was completed?

After his death his body was put in a nearby tomb made available by a wealthy and respected supporter. He had come out into the open at the very time when many of Christ's followers had run for cover. The full embalming of the body was postponed for two days when a group of women—including Jesus' mother—had agreed to visit the tomb and treat the body according to the custom of the time. When, at dawn two days later, the women arrived they found the tomb empty.

They went rushing back to the grief stricken, but now reunited, group of followers. They came with the astonishing claim that they had not only found the tomb empty but that they had met 'angels' at the tomb who stated that Jesus had been raised from the dead.

Not surprisingly the others refused to believe such wild claims. Two men who had been particularly close to Jesus ran to the tomb. What they found perplexed them.

The body and head wrappings which had been wound round the body were still in the tomb and on the ledge where the body had been laid. The amazing thing was—*the wrappings were still wrapped*! It was as if the body had simply evaporated inside, leaving those wrappings flat on the ledge.

Then came the reports—from one person here and another there. Jesus had been seen again. Somehow different and yet clearly the same. The followers gathered to discuss the bewildering situation—*and there was Jesus, appearing in the room alongside his old friends.*

For several weeks these strange appearances took place. Sometimes Jesus spent several hours with a group of his followers talking over the significance of all that had happened. There were no doubts now. Luke wrote: 'he showed himself to these men and gave many convincing proofs that he was alive.' The despair and grief were forgotten. Something new and astonishing was happening!

One of the themes that the risen Jesus hammered home to those first followers was this—they had a story to tell to the world. They were his witnesses. The life, death and resurrection of Jesus was the key to the meaning of everything else. God had broken into time and space. People needed to know. They needed to change their minds about what really matters, *and to believe in Jesus*.

More than that. Those followers, and others who would later believe the story they had to tell, had to carry on where Jesus had left off. Did Jesus live unselfishly with a concern for the welfare of others? *So must they*. That showed what life was like when the true King ruled.

Did Jesus forgive those who harmed him—including the soldiers who nailed him to the cross? *So must they*.

Did Jesus bring peace, and healing to the broken bodies and broken relationships. *So must they*.

Did Jesus single out and care for the weak, the poor, the undervalued (including, in those times, women and children)? *So must they*.

Was Jesus described as a friend of sinners? *So too must his followers be described.*

What Jesus said to his followers, soon after he had risen from the grave, summed up the whole challenge: '*As the Father sent me, so I send you.*'

Then came the day when the appearances of Jesus stopped. On a hill close to Jerusalem the risen Christ was caught up in a cloud and left his loyal followers. They knew it was the end of that chapter of the story. He had left them immediately after telling them to go and tell the story to people of every sort and in every place.

Ever since that day people, in increasing numbers throughout the world, have become caught up in the continuing story of Jesus. They believe he was and is the 'son of God' who directly broke into time and space. They believe that he has shown us what God is like and how we should live. They see in him how much God loves and forgives us even when our lives fall well short of his standards.

And the story isn't over yet. It will end when God brings down the final curtain on history and when all of us will have to face him and answer for the lives we have lived.

Ever since I can remember I have been aware of the Jesus story and, more-or-less, believed it. There are many like me. It was in my early teenage years, however, that I became convinced that the story of Jesus was not only true but that I was meant to 'join the cast of millions' and become part of the action. It was now *my* story as well as his.

This booklet is written to encourage others to become 'people of the story' or *Christians*. The big thing about being a Christian is not the Church label or tradition to which we belong (important though that may be). It is believing that *the story is true and that it is still going on with people like us playing our parts within it.*

■ What does the story mean?

I believe that the story of Jesus is true—it actually happened, resurrection and all. But so what? The world is full of stories. I believe we need to ask *what does the story mean*? What does it tell us about life; about God and about people? The first Christians drew several conclusions as they thought about Jesus. Here are some of them.

1. There is a God

In fact, the first Christians didn't need much persuading on that one! Things are different now. We can explain a tremendous amount about life, our origins, the universe and so on. Many today don't feel the need to call in some sort of God to explain why we are here.

But the truth is not whether we feel the need for a God of some sort. The truth is that Jesus demonstrated *there is a God*. We may be able to explain a great deal of the *how* of our origins. Jesus showed us the *why*. His resurrection pointed to something 'out of this world' about him. He himself constantly spoke of a 'Father' from whom he had come and who cared deeply for each one of us. His coming into space and time was a message saying: 'God exists'. For me this means we are not meaningless specks of life on a puzzling planet. We are people who matter, made ultimately by a Father God who obviously wants us to be here and to be on the receiving end of his love.

2. This God loves me

We didn't have to exist but we do! We're here because God wants us. Jesus didn't have to come into our world and face the suspicion and hatred of people and that cruel death. But he did. 'God loved the world so much that he gave his only Son . . .' wrote John.

The way Jesus lived. His weeping alongside the bereaved. His determination to heal. His love of children and the moving stories he told—all this underlined the convictions of the first Christians that God cares. No one he met was too corrupt, too immoral or too evil for him not to show love and the readiness to forgive.

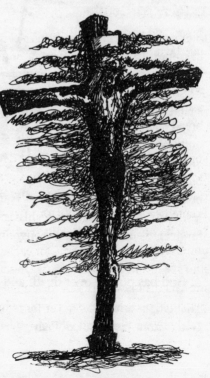

Finally there was the cross. Jesus said that he was laying down his life for his friends. We are loved.

3. We can be forgiven

Wherever Jesus went he talked about people's need for forgiveness. No matter what problem people thought they were bringing to him, Jesus usually started by forgiving their sins. *The first Christians saw that forgiveness for our inbuilt wrongfulness and self-centredness is where we all have to start with God.*

As time passed the first Christians saw more clearly that the death on the cross was at the centre of the story of Jesus and the story of their own lives.

Just before his arrest, Jesus had taken bread and wine at a meal with his closest followers. As he shared it around he said that the broken bread and the outpoured wine were like his own body and blood—broken and poured out to give life for others. Human wrongfulness put Jesus on the cross but through his death Jesus had made the forgiveness of our human wrongfulness possible.

4. God has power over death and over evil

That empty tomb was never forgotten. It revealed that the God, whom Jesus called 'Father', had the power to defeat death. But there was more. It revealed that *human beings* can be raised from death. For us there can be life after death. One of the first Christians wrote the following words in a letter to his friends: ' . . . the truth is that Christ has been raised from death, as the guarantee that those who sleep in death will also be raised . . . where, Death, is your victory?'

For so many people, the certainty of death is the ultimate area of fear. It also makes many wonder whether life has any real point or purpose. Are all our efforts simply to end with a great jump into nothingness—or perhaps even worse?

The story of Jesus gives us hope to believe that what lies beyond the grave is better than anything to be found before we get there.

The resurrection of Jesus means more than the promise of life after death for those who take sides with Jesus. It shows that—in spite of appearances—God is ultimately in charge. He will bring about what he wants in the end.

Those of us who write ourselves into the ongoing story of Jesus will not escape hard times, opposition and even danger, but God is with us and he is in control of history. His plans for a 'heaven' will not be shaken. It will be a world where peace and justice dominate and where all who care about Jesus and what he represents will find an eternal home. Evil will be defeated.

5. God can be with us now

What soon became clear after the final disappearance of the

risen Jesus was that *he had not really left them*. Jesus had talked about 'another helper' taking over after he had left his followers. He called that other helper 'the Spirit who reveals the truth about God'.

One of the most famous early Christians talked about 'the Spirit of Christ' and said that through this Spirit 'Christ is in you'. He and others of his time, and since, spoke of the Spirit being 'in' us as well as 'alongside' us.

As someone who stepped into the Jesus story many years ago I cannot pretend that I have always felt that Christ has been near me. But the overwhelming reality in my life—in spite of occasional times of uncertainty—has been that Christ has kept his promise to me. He said 'I will be with you always'. For me the story goes on being true.

I have written this booklet because I want others to make the same discovery.

■ Where do we go from here?

People respond to the story of Jesus in several ways. I find people saying something like the following:

1. *'I don't believe it'*

It is not surprising that a fair number of people find the story of Jesus unbelievable. With talk of a son of God coming into the world; people rising from the dead; miracles and demons—it all seems to belong more to the world of fairy tales than to the world of truth and hard facts.

On the other hand some of the most intelligent people who have ever lived are amongst those who *do* believe! We need to ask *why* we say we don't believe. Is it because it would upset our way of life? If so—that is not an intelligent reason. Is it because we find the story unbelievable? Again we must ask *why*?

The thing we must face is that we all tend to jump off from fixed positions when we do our thinking and we rarely think about those fixed positions—the things we take for granted. If someone starts from a fixed belief that miracles don't happen then obviously the story of Jesus is unbelievable. But *why* are we saying miracles don't happen? The Jesus story challenges us to ask serious questions about what we take for granted.

2. 'Yes, it may well be true but I don't want to think about it now'

Again I would want to ask *why* don't you want to think about it now? If it is true, surely the sooner we get stuck into it, the better.

We are creatures of habit and habits get a grip on us. We can form a habit of putting off deciding about Christ and such a habit could become unbreakable.

3. 'I wish I could believe it but I still have difficulties and uncertainties'

This is a very honest position to take. There *are* difficulties. Most Christians themselves go through times when they hit doubts and problems with some part of the story or concerning how to relate the story to life. For all the talk of God's Holy Spirit and of Christ being near to us, there are times when little seems to go right and God seems very far away.

I would want to say to people who feel they can't 'buy the whole package'—I'm glad you are interested and feel drawn. That's very important. There are two things more:

◆ Believe what you *can* believe for the present.
◆ Keep yourself open to the possibility of understanding more.

There are many people in our churches who still have doubts and uncertainties. The exciting thing is that they want to have doubts as *insiders*! Churches are meant to be places where everyone is a learner. There are no short cuts. One of the earliest Christian leaders wrote: 'we are being changed from one degree of glory to another.' Jesus was surrounded by people who were still feeling their way towards full faith in him. Why should it be different today?

4. '*I believe it and I want to know that I'm in!*'

Over the years I have come to see that it is a help to many people in this position to be able to *mark the moment*. Perhaps it's similar to people getting married. In one sense they don't need a ceremony to mark the moment of starting the relationship but the ceremony marks the moment. In later years they look back with warm feelings concerning the wedding day.

The best way I know to *mark the moment* of believing and becoming part of the continuing story of Jesus is to say a simple prayer, very deliberately, as a commitment to God. It may help to say it in the presence of another Christian. Here is a suggested prayer.

Dear Father

Thank you for your love for me. Thank you for giving me life and thank you for sending Jesus Christ to help me to see your love and concern.

I admit that I have stayed away from you and from what you wanted for my life. Please forgive me.

Thank you that Jesus died for all that is wrong in my life so that I can be forgiven and become your son/ daughter.

Please send your Holy Spirit into my life to make me new. Help me to know that you are near and help me to grow more like Jesus.

And now I give my word that I will join with your Son, and with those who believe in him, in serving you and caring for the world around me.

Amen.

■ A final thought

Marking the moment with a prayer or in any other way is not like some magic charm. Just as saying vows at the wedding service doesn't guarantee that the marriage will be successful, so resolutions about God need to be followed by action.

Every Christian needs to belong to a Christian congregation. At times it needs patience with others but then they will need patience with us!

The two most important things to remember are first that Christ has much to teach us and not just at head level. There may well have to be some changes!

The second thing to remember is best put in the words of Jesus himself:

'Everyone whom my Father gives me will come to me. I will never turn away anyone who comes to me.'

Signing on

Today I decided to mark the moment of coming to believe that the story of Jesus is true. I want to be part of the story from this moment onwards.

Signature . . . .   Date . . . .

Stories that Jesus told

Some Bible notes by Shelagh Brown

Introduction

A professor of theology once climbed up into the pulpit of a college chapel in Oxford. He had been commissioned to preach the special, annual sermon to the bedmakers and the college servants. He gazed down at them from his ivory tower and began:

'I expect,' he said, 'that you have given a great deal of thought to the ontological argument for the existence of God ...'

But I think it is very unlikely that they had! And Jesus would never have started a sermon in such a silly way. His way of telling us the truth about God for all time was totally different.

He watched ordinary people doing ordinary things, and then he taught us and showed us what God is like through the things that we know. Perhaps as a small child he watched his mother putting raw dough from the last batch of bread-making into the new batch—and stood wide-eyed as the bread doubled its volume and rose up—all because of

the tiny piece of leavened dough that she had kneaded into
it, and that now he couldn't see. Then, later on, when he
began his ministry, the bread and the yeast was at the heart
of one of his stories about God and the kingdom of God.

Jesus would have gazed at the vines growing in the
fields—with their twisted thin branches—and seen the

bunches of beautiful, sweet grapes growing on the branches. He would have watched the fierce pruning earlier in the year that the vinedresser had given to make the vine bear a heavy crop of fruit. And he would have seen shepherds looking after their flocks, and perhaps helped them to rescue their sheep when they strayed away and got lost. He would have known the preciousness of water in that dry and thirsty land, and he would have known the darkness of the night and the light of the day.

The stories and the parables of Jesus are unique. They show us God in a way that speaks right to our hearts, and they can show us how our story fits into his story. So here are some of the best-known stories that Jesus ever told. The religious leaders hated his stories, but the ordinary people and the outcasts of society loved them.

Stories
that
Jesus
told

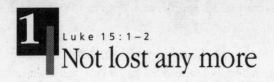

1 Not lost any more

Now the tax collectors and 'sinners' were all gathering round to hear [Jesus]. But the Pharisees and the teachers of the law muttered, 'This man welcomes sinners, and eats with them.'

This whole chapter from Luke's Gospel, which we shall look at for the next few days, is all about lost things and lost people. It starts with a criticism of Jesus. But what the Pharisees said about him is very good news for those of us who know that we have often acted wrongfully and that we're sinners.

A Christian friend of mine who is an alcoholic once said to me: 'I shall never be able to say, "I *was* an alcoholic." I *am* one, and I always shall be. And it's like that with being a sinner, isn't it?'

But there is all the difference in the world between sinners who don't know they are (like the Pharisees) and sinners who do know, and who have been and are being forgiven.

The tax collectors and prostitutes whom Jesus received and ate with were sinners. But the story says that a lot of them were forgiven sinners. Once they were lost, but now they were found—by the Saviour of the world who had come to do just that. 'The Son of man is come to seek and to save that which is lost . . .'

A lost thing isn't fulfilling its purpose. When I lose my stamps (which usually live under a tray on my hall table, but sometimes stray into other places where I can't find them) they cannot be stuck on my letters to show the Post Office that I have paid the price of the postage.

When people are lost they aren't fulfilling their purpose either—which is to be a son or a daughter of God, and to live in a loving relationship with God for ever and ever. The Westminster Confession, one of the Church's statements about the purpose of life, says that 'the chief end of man is to know God and to enjoy him for ever'.

Now the tax collectors and the sinners were starting to know God, and God in Christ was sitting down at table and eating with them. And telling them stories the like of which they had never heard before.

A prayer

Jesus, Saviour of the world, I am so glad that you welcome sinners and eat with them—and that you welcome me. Let me listen to the stories you told us, so that I can know what God is really like.

2
Luke 15:3–6
The found sheep

Then Jesus told them this parable: 'Suppose one of you has a hundred sheep and loses one of them. Does he not leave the ninety-nine in the open country and go after the lost sheep until he finds it? And when he finds it, he joyfully puts it on his shoulders and goes home. Then he calls his friends and neighbours together and says, "Rejoice with me; I have found my lost sheep." I tell you that in the same way there will be more rejoicing in heaven over one sinner who repents than over ninety-nine righteous persons who do not need to repent.'

This chapter of Luke has been called 'the gospel within the gospel.' The stories in it astonish us and delight us with the tenderness and the love of God, who searches after the lost until he finds them.

It was tough going to find a lost sheep in parts of Palestine. In Judea there was a central plateau to graze on that was only a few miles wide, and at the end of it were steep cliffs and a terrible desert. Sheep have a tendency to wander off and get lost (and Jesus said that we are like them!)—and when the shepherd counted up his flock and found that there were only ninety-nine he went off into the wilderness to find the lost one.

The shepherd was an expert in tracking—and he followed the footmarks all the way that the sheep had taken, going right to the very edges of the safe places to graze. Perhaps this one had fallen down the cliff, or strayed into the desert where there were no green pastures and no still waters to drink from. The sheep would be lonely—dumbly aware that it was separated from the sheep in the flock, and that the shepherd wasn't there.

But then the sheep would hear the voice of the shepherd, the voice it knew so well. And perhaps it would bleat in reply. The strong shepherd would gather the lost, tired sheep into his arms, and put it on his shoulder, and carry it home again. And the shepherd would be glad, and so would the sheep.

A prayer

Lord Jesus Christ, you said that you are the good shepherd. Thank you that you mind about the sheep who gets lost—and that you go out to find it. Into all the desolate places of our world—the rich and the desolate places where the sheep is lost, and the poor and desolate places . . .

3 The found coin

'Or suppose a woman has ten silver coins and loses one. Does she not light a lamp, sweep the house and search carefully until she finds it? And when she finds it, she calls her friends and neighbours together and says, "Rejoice with me; I have found my lost coin." In the same way, I tell you, there is rejoicing in the presence of the angels of God over one sinner who repents.'

Two days ago I dropped a penny on the floor of the bus when the driver gave me my change. I didn't get down and look for it, because a penny is worth so little. But the coin that this woman was looking for was of great value. It was made of silver, so it might just have been an ordinary coin—a drachma, which was more than a day's wages. The loss of it might have meant that the family got no supper. This coin may have been the only money that this woman had—except that she didn't have it. It was lost. So in the darkness of a house with tiny windows, and in the dried reeds on a floor of beaten earth, the woman looked and swept—until she saw the gleam of silver and gave a cry of delight.

The delight might have been because it was a different kind of coin. In those days a married woman wore a headdress of ten silver coins hanging on a silver chain. A girl would save for years to buy them, and they were almost the equivalent of a wedding ring. She would still have had the nine silver coins on the silver chain—but one was lost, so it wasn't complete or perfect any more. Like an engagement ring out of which one stone is lost—and the space shows more than the stones which are left. But the woman found her coin—and she was very, very glad.

A prayer

Lord God, I love it that you are glad when one sinner repents—and that the angels in heaven are full of joy. I am glad that you are the God you are—like a shepherd who goes out to look for a lost sheep, and like a woman who sweeps and searches for a lost coin. I am glad that your Son came to seek and to save the lost—and that includes me. Now I pray for those whom I know and love who seem to be lost, and ask that you will find them...

4

The lost son

Jesus continued: 'There was a man who had two sons. The younger one said to his father, "Father, give me my share of the estate." So he divided his property between them.

'Not long after that, the younger son got together all he had, set off for a distant country and there squandered his wealth in wild living. After he had spent everything, there was a severe famine in that whole country, and he began to be in need. So he went and hired himself out to a citizen of that country, who sent him to his fields to feed pigs. He longed to fill his stomach with the pods that the pigs were eating, but no-one gave him anything.

'When he came to his senses, he said, "How many of my father's hired men have food to spare, and here I am starving to death! I will set out and go back to my father and say to him: Father, I have sinned against heaven and against you. I am no longer worthy to be called your son; make me like one of your hired men." So he got up and went to his father.'

The story that we shall be looking at for the next three days has been called the greatest short story in the world. When a father died his eldest son was entitled to two-thirds of the estate and the younger son one third. But this younger son had demanded it now—and he took it with him and spent it. All of it. On loose living. And his money and the food of the country ran out at the same time and there was a famine. He ended up in a field feeding pigs. They were fed but he was hungry, and his hunger brought him to his senses.

I once saw Britten's *The Prodigal Son* in a church. There was only one prop. A large, yellow sun made of cardboard hung on a pole with a pulley behind it. When the prodigal son left home the cardboard yellow sun, at the top of the pole, started to get lower and lower until it reached the bottom. Then, when the son decided to go home, the cardboard sun started to rise again.

A prayer

Father, if I am in a far country, draw me home again... Make me come to my senses.

5

The waiting father

'But while he was still a long way off, his father saw him and was filled with compassion for him; he ran to his son, threw his arms around him and kissed him.

'The son said to him, "Father, I have sinned against heaven and against you. I am no longer worthy to be called your son."

'But the father said to his servants, "Quick! Bring the best robe and put it on him. Put a ring on his finger and sandals on his feet. Bring the fattened calf and kill it. Let's have a feast and celebrate. For this son of mine was dead and is alive again; he was lost and is found." So they began to celebrate.'

We usually call this the story of the prodigal son. But a famous preacher and theologian, Helmut Thielicke, called it the story of the waiting father—because it is the father who is right at the heart of it. The father who watches with a heavy heart as his son goes away—and who waits with a longing heart for him to come home again. When the son does come home the father is looking out for him. He sees him a long way off and he runs out to meet him. Perhaps he had to pick up the skirts of his robe as he ran—full of love and compassion for the scruffy son who is coming home again. The son confesses his sins to his father—sins against the father and against heaven—but the father doesn't talk about them. He clothes him in the best robe (a mark of honour) and gives him a ring (perhaps the signet ring which was the power of attorney). Then they have a feast.

The Scottish minister and Bible scholar William Barclay says that 'Jesus paid sinning humanity the greatest compliment it has ever been paid. "When he came to himself he said . . . " Jesus believed that so long as a man was away from God he was not truly himself; he was only truly himself when he was on the way home . . . He believed that man was never essentially himself until he came home to God.'

A prayer

Father God, I run into your open arms—knowing that you run out to meet me. I marvel at that—and I delight in your great love, and your great tenderness, and your great glory.

Luke 15:25–32
Lost at home

'Meanwhile, the older son was in the field. When he came near the house, he heard music and dancing. So he called one of the servants and asked him what was going on. "Your brother has come," he replied, "and your father has killed the fattened calf because he has him back safe and sound."

'The older brother became angry and refused to go in. So his father went out and pleaded with him. But he answered his father, "Look! All these years I've been slaving for you and never disobeyed your orders. Yet you never gave me even a young goat so I could celebrate with my friends. But when this son of yours who has squandered your property with prostitutes comes home, you kill the fattened calf for him!"

' "My son," the father said, "you are always with me, and everything I have is yours. But we had to celebrate and be glad, because this brother of yours was dead and is alive again; he was lost and is found." '

It can't have been easy for the eldest son. He was at home in the father's house, but he wasn't really enjoying it. He can't have been. Otherwise he wouldn't have been angry. Not if he had been delighting in the happiness of home, with the close, loving Jewish family around him—and work to do, day by day, on the land that the Jews loved and counted so precious. When Isaac was blessing Jacob (who was pretending to be Esau and wearing his clothes) he said, 'the smell of my son is like the smell of a field'—and he delighted in the smell of it. The rich fragrance of the earth; the fragrance of warm, dry hay; and the sweet smell of cows...

A Jew loved the land—but this Jewish son didn't. Not very much. And he didn't love his father very much either. If he had he would have been delighting in all the years he had spent at home in the father's house, in the father's presence, and in the fellowship and friendship of the father's family. He would have pitied his brother for the years he had lost away from the father. Perhaps, when he saw his younger brother enjoying all that the father had to give him, he had his own change of heart and came back from his own far country—inside his own lost heart.

7
John 4:7–10
Living water

When a Samaritan woman came to draw water, Jesus said to her, 'Will you give me a drink?' (His disciples had gone into the town to buy food.) The Samaritan woman said to him, 'You are a Jew and I am a Samaritan woman. How can you ask me for a drink?' (For Jews do not associate with Samaritans.) Jesus answered her, 'If you knew the gift of God and who it is that asks you for a drink, you would have asked him and he would have given you living water.'

Have you ever experienced a yearning and a longing deep inside you that is like a thirst, but that neither water nor wine would ever satisfy? A yearning and a thirsting for something—you don't really know what it is, and yet in one way you do know. It is a thirst for a total quenching of the thirst of your soul. We all thirst like that sometimes, but we don't all recognize it for what it is. The only water that will ever quench it is the living God who is living water.

People at the top of society's heap get just as thirsty as those at the bottom of it, but the woman at Samaria was fairly near the bottom. Perhaps she was getting water in the heat of the day because the respectable women of the village disapproved of her lifestyle. Jacob's well was a mile away from her village, and she was tired. Campbell Morgan says that she was 'degraded, disillusioned and dissatisfied'; we could just say 'thirsty'. Then she meets Jesus: 'He was face to face with a thirsty woman, and offered himself to her as being able to quench that thirst, and that meant able to lift her from the degradation into which she had fallen; able to give to her, who had become disillusioned, an entirely new outlook upon life; able to come to the deep, scorching, burning, restless dissatisfaction, and bring her complete satisfaction!'

A prayer

Lord Jesus Christ, I come to you with the thirst that is inside me. You know the bitter waters that I have drunk in the past, that have never quenched my thirst. You know the sweet waters of success that I have sometimes drunk, that haven't quenched my inner thirst either. I come to you and drink.

8
The river of life

On the last and greatest day of the Feast, Jesus stood and said in a loud voice, 'If anyone is thirsty, let him come to me and drink. Whoever believes in me, as the Scripture has said, streams of living water will flow from within him.' By this he meant the Spirit, whom those who believed in him were later to receive. Up to that time the Spirit had not been given, since Jesus had not been glorified.

A Jewish prophet, Ezekiel, once saw a vision of the river of life that flows from the throne of God. It gets deeper all the way— and in Ezekiel's vision a man tells him that when the river 'enters the stagnant waters of the sea the sea will become fresh. And wherever the river goes every living creature which swarms will live, and there will be many fish; for this water goes there, that the waters of the sea may become fresh; so everything will live where the river goes' (Ezekiel 47:8–9).

Imagine having a river like that in our polluted world with its poisoned seas. A river of life that flows into the damaged places and makes them whole. That flows into the dead places and makes them alive. A river that flows into dirty, degraded and sad souls and washes them clean and makes them alive with the life of God.

That is what Jesus offers us—if we want it. If we thirst for it. First of all the washing and the healing of our own souls. Then the flowing out of the river of life through us into the world that he loves and that he died for.

It starts with those who believe in Jesus: 'Those who have come to Him, and have had their own thirst quenched, that is to know what it means to have received the gift of the living water, that has become in them a well of water, springing up, laughing up, bubbling up, for ever springing, beautifying, satisfying...' (Dr Campbell Morgan). And then the river of life flows out of us—living water for a dead world.

A prayer

Lord Jesus Christ, I believe in you. I come to you and I drink—and I believe your promise that out of me, and out of all who believe in you, rivers of living water will flow into your polluted, damaged, beloved world.

9

Matthew 13:33
Powerful stuff

He told them still another parable: 'The kingdom of heaven is like yeast that a woman took and mixed into a large amount of flour until it worked all through the dough.'

If you have ever made bread you will know about the amazing qualities of yeast. The tiny spores of a fungus, it can live in a dry state for years (mine lives in a blue tin in my refrigerator), but when it is given the right food and the right conditions it will start to grow. I put a tablespoon of the dried yeast into a small bowl with a teaspoonful of sugar and some warm water—and within minutes things start to happen. There is an unmistakable smell, and a pale brown, frothy mixture visibly increasing in my bowl.

Then I add that to three pounds of stoneground flour and two pints of warm water and knead it. I cannot see the yeast any more—but it is still there, still working, invisible and powerful. The dough that half-filled my bread tins rises to the rim of them—then I put the loaves into the oven and bake them for 45 minutes—and usually cut off a crust and butter it and eat it while it is still hot.

In Jesus' day they didn't have dried yeast in little blue tins. His mother would have kept back one piece of raw, leavened dough to put in the next batch of bread that she made—and the effect would start all over again. The tiny yeast, or leaven, transforms the whole of the bread it is put into. And the kingdom of heaven is like that.

It affects the whole of society. Society's attitude to sick people and old people was transformed by the yeast of the kingdom. It was Christianity that started to look after the poor and the ill and the old. William Barclay, a Scottish minister and a Bible scholar, said that 'Christianity was the first faith to be interested in the broken things of life'.

A prayer

Lord Jesus, I thank you for the powerful changes that the kingdom of God works in the whole of society—in broken lives and in evil places. Show me what I can do to work with you in the work of your kingdom.

10

John 6 : 48–51
Living bread

'I am the bread of life. Your forefathers ate the manna in the desert, yet they died. But here is the bread that comes down from heaven, which a man may eat and not die. I am the living bread that came down from heaven. If anyone eats of this bread, he will live for ever. This bread is my flesh, which I will give for the life of the world.'

'Bread' is our basic food, the starchy stuff that we cannot live without. Perhaps it is a plate of pasta or maize porridge, a bowl of rice or a crusty loaf.

In Jesus' day the bread was made of barley or wheat—and in the East bread was sacred. It still is. When people broke bread with one another it was a sign of hospitality and friendship. The one who provided the bread gave the hospitality. Those who ate it were united in fellowship with each other and with their host.

When Jesus spoke about bread, those are the things that his listeners would have understood. And they knew that bread had to be eaten if it was going to do them any good. Bread was for nourishing them and for keeping them alive. When they were hungry they wanted bread.

One day by the Sea of Galilee Jesus fed five thousand

people with bread and fishes. The next day they followed him to the other side of the sea hoping for more. But he didn't give them any more. Instead, he gave them a profound lesson in theology and spirituality, and he used the ordinary bread they had eaten to lead them to an understanding of who he was.

'I am the bread of life'—and to say 'I am' was to say what his nature was—just as God had revealed his nature to Moses by telling him his name: 'I am who I am' . . . The one who is, and who exists: who always has and who always will. The one who is the eternal Lord God and whom to know is eternal life. The one on whose eternal being we can feed. The one who is the bread of life to us. Jesus Christ.

The bread of Holy Communion is an outward and visible sign of an inward, invisible grace. The sacrament that we share is an eating with our bodies that is a sign of the feeding of our souls. Not just on Sundays—but all the time. We feed on the being of Jesus Christ, God incarnate.

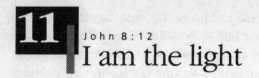

11
I am the light

When Jesus spoke again to the people, he said, 'I am the light of the world. Whoever follows me will never walk in darkness, but will have the light of life.'

Jesus is speaking to the people, but the Pharisees are listening to him too—and they don't like what he says. Jesus tells them that he is the light of the world. But they hated the light—and in the darkness of a Friday morning they arranged to have it put out.

But in the glory of Easter morning the light shone out again—and the risen Christ appeared to his astonished, terrified and delighted followers. He doesn't appear to us in the same way. But he still calls us to follow him, and he still makes the same promises.

You probably know Holman Hunt's painting 'The Light of the World'. Christ is standing outside a house and knocking on the door. There is no handle on the outside, because if Christ is to go inside the owner of the house will have to open the door and invite him in.

Years ago, when my life was in a dreadful mess and I was deeply unhappy, a curate called John Collins told me about that picture. He said that if I would ask Christ into my heart he would change my life and forgive my sins. So I went home, knelt by my bed, and read out the verse John had given me: 'Behold, I stand at the door and knock; if any one hears my voice and opens the door, I will come in to him and eat with him, and he with me' (Revelation 3:20). Then I prayed, 'Lord, I open the door of my heart now. Please come in.'

I know that he did, because I knew then (with a deep certainty that nothing has ever been able to shake) that God is my Father, that he loves me, and that my sins are forgiven. I have sometimes prayed the prayer since—asking Christ to enter rooms in the house of my life that I had kept locked. But that first prayer totally changed my life.

A way to pray

Sit in silence and let the light of Christ shine into your heart—and into every room in the house of your life. Then, if you are willing, invite him to come in—perhaps for the first time, or perhaps into places where you have never allowed him to enter before.

Come into the light

For God so loved the world that he gave his one and only Son, that whoever believes in him shall not perish but have eternal life. For God did not send his Son into the world to condemn the world, but to save the world through him. Whoever believes in him is not condemned, but whoever does not believe stands condemned already because he has not believed in the name of God's one and only Son. This is the verdict: Light has come into the world, but men loved darkness instead of light because their deeds were evil. Everyone who does evil hates the light, and will not come into the light for fear that his deeds will be exposed. But whoever lives by the truth comes into the light, so that it may be seen plainly that what he has done has been done through God.

When my friends come to supper I light my room with the soft glow of candlelight, backed up by the low light of 25-watt bulbs in table lamps. Everything looks beautiful (even us!) because candlelight is a gentle light.

But when I want to clean my house I draw my curtains right back and let the light of day shine into all the hidden places: the corners where the spiders have made their webs and the places under furniture where I discover peanuts and paper clips.

We see how things really are in a clear, bright light—not in a dim light or in the darkness. So what happens when we come into the light of God? Well, we see ourselves as we really are. We see that we're not very good at loving, even the people we love most, and that we are not what we should be. But we also begin to see God as he really is. It starts to dawn on us, like the warmth of the sun's rising, that the light shining into our hearts is the light of love. And just as I let the light of day shine into my room when I want to clean it, so does God shine his light into our hearts. He cleans them by forgiving our sins, and then comes and live in them. So long as we will come to the light and let him do it.

A prayer

Eternal Light, shine into my heart and let me see myself. Then let me see your glory and your love shining in the face of Jesus Christ.

13

A debt wiped out

'A certain creditor had two debtors; one owed five hundred denarii, and the other fifty. When they could not pay, he forgave them both. Now which of them will love him more?' Simon answered, 'The one I suppose, to whom he forgave more.' And he said to him, 'You have judged rightly.'

Jesus had gone to dinner in the house of a Pharisee called Simon. In the normal course of events in an eastern household the host would have had water to wash his guest's feet, oil to anoint his head—and he would have greeted his guest with a kiss. Simon did none of these things. But then a woman comes in who is a prostitute and she does all the things that Simon should have done. She washes his feet with her tears, dries them with her hair, and anoints them with the most precious thing she has—the perfumed, concentrated oil that she wore around her neck, as all Jewish women did, in a little phial known as an alabaster. And she kissed his feet and went on kissing them. All Simon did was to disapprove—and think in his heart that if Jesus really was a prophet he would have known that the woman was a prostitute and therefore defiling him by her touch. But Simon had it hopelessly wrong. Jesus by his touch had made the woman clean and whole. She knew his cleansing and his forgiveness. Jesus had reached her heart—and then he tried to reach Simon's. That is what our passage is about.

In Britain in the 1990s debts and creditors are the common currency of life. Creditors very rarely forgive people's debts—what usually happens is that they move in to possess goods and property. But imagine that one incredible morning the credit company sends round their representative and tells first a person who owes them for a Hoover, and then a person who owes them for a house, that there is nothing to pay. The representative says to each of them, 'We forgive you your debt...' The person who now owns the vacuum cleaner will be pleased enough. But think of the person who now owns their house.

A prayer

Lord Jesus Christ, thank you for paying the debt of my sin.

14

Washing and wine

On the third day a wedding took place at Cana in Galilee. Jesus' mother was there, and Jesus and his disciples had also been invited to the wedding. When the wine was gone, Jesus' mother said to him, 'They have no more wine.' 'Dear woman, why do you involve me?' Jesus replied, 'My time has not yet come.' His mother said to the servants, 'Do whatever he tells you.' Nearby stood six stone water jars, the kind used by the Jews for ceremonial washing, each holding from twenty to thirty gallons. Jesus said to the servants, 'Fill the jars with water'; so they filled them to the brim. Then he told them, 'Now draw some out and take it to the master of the banquet.' They did so, and the master of the banquet tasted the water that had been turned into wine ... Then he called the bridegroom aside and said, 'Everyone brings out the choice wine first and then the cheaper wine after the guests have had too much too drink; but you have saved the best till now.'

Water is for washing in as well as for drinking–and those great water-pots standing there in the wedding feast were the ones to hold the water for the Jewish ceremonial washings. The outer washing in Christian baptism is the symbol of an inward washing. The inside of us has to be washed as well as the outside, and the inside washing matters far more.

It cannot have been by accident that Jesus did his first miracle by using those particular waterpots. 'Fill the jars with water'—and they did what he told them (and must have been a bit perplexed.) 'Now draw some out and take it to the master of the banquet.' The water that was for outward washing was going to be drunk, so that the inside was washed as well as the outside. But the water turned into wine. This wine was out of the ordinary even on a human level. The master, or the steward, knew better than anyone there what good wine tasted like. This was the best wine. On a spiritual level it is the transformation from outward washing to the inner quenching of a spiritual thirst, with the water of washing turned into the wine of joy.

A prayer

Lord Jesus Christ, may I know the miracle within me of water turned into wine ... of ordinary things touched by you, and blessed to me, so that they delight me and make me intoxicated with you. Touch all the circumstances of my life— including the sad ones—so that I may receive them as the wine of eternal life.

If you have enjoyed reading and using *Our Place in His Story*, you may wish to know that similar material is available from BRF in a regular series of Bible reading notes, *New Daylight*, which is published three times a year (in January, May and September) and contains printed Bible passages, brief comments and prayers. *New Daylight* is also available in a large print version.

Copies of *New Daylight* may be obtained from your local Christian bookshop or by subscription direct from BRF (see subscription order form opposite).

For more information about *New Daylight* and the full range of BRF publications, write to: The Bible Reading Fellowship, Peter's Way, Sandy Lane West, OXFORD OX4 5HG (Tel: 0865 748227)

SUBSCRIPTION ORDER FORM

Please send me the following, beginning with the Jan/May/Sep* issue:

Qty			Total £
___	New Daylight	£8.25 p.a.	_____
___	New Daylight Large Print	£12.00 p.a.	_____

* delete as appropriate

All prices include postage and packing

Please complete the payment details below—all orders must be accompanied by the appropriate payment—and send your completed order to **BRF, Peter's Way, Sandy Lane West, Oxford, OX4 5HG**

Name: ....

Address:..

....

....

Signed: .... Date: ....

Payment for subscription(s) £..

Donation £...

Total enclosed £...

Payment by Cheque☐ Postal Order☐ Visa☐ Mastercard☐

Expiry Date of Card..

Signature ....
(essential if paying by credit card)

Information and prices are guaranteed until 31/12/94 BRF is a Reg. Charity (No. 233280)